Table of Contents

Introduction

You have probably heard the word "intelligence," and maybe you even equate it to someone's education. However, have you heard of "emotional intelligence?" The chances are that you have a vague idea about what this is all about, but if you are lacking in self-confidence or find yourself becoming too emotional in different situations that are presented to you, you are not making the most of the potential of emotional intelligence.

This book was written because I am on a mission. That mission is to help people to gain a better knowledge of what emotional intelligence is all about because it can improve their lives beyond all recognition. We all have emotions. These are the thoughts and the feelings that swing our lives up and down and even find us lost for words or generally lost or confused. However, when you learn to use emotions intelligently, you can actually start to gain confidence and take control of your life. Don't believe me? Then you need to look into the pages of this book, as it may hold answers that you haven't even thought of.

How would I know? I have worked with people from all walks of life and have experienced the mixed bag of emotions that people experience every day of my working life. Having been aware of how people's viewpoints are stilted by their emotions, I thought it a good time to put pen to paper and help those who are finding this particular balancing act hard to control. This is your chance to shine and all you need to do is read and take notice of the chapters that lie ahead. When you do, you will surprise yourself because all you needed was guidance. Taking the right direction gets you there quickly while most people these days seem to prefer their lives to be hit and miss and end up stressed and out of control of their lives. Want all that to change? Then read on, and you will learn how to do just that.

Do try to change things in your way of thinking and use the exercises in the book to help you to do that. Then you will be happier and happier people are more productive and confident people, who give more to their lives and get so much more back.

Chapter 1: What is Emotional Intelligence?

When it comes to being successful, one of the most important qualities you can possess is emotional intelligence. Emotional intelligence is to be self-aware of your own emotions and to be able to manage and control them in your personal and professional lives. To be able to harness your emotions in a potential crisis is a valuable quality to have, especially in a professional setting.

Staying cool, calm, and collected will help you to apply your strong emotions toward problem solving and critical thinking. This is key when running your own business, managing a number of people, or even just becoming a better team player by acting quickly, rather than rationally, and solving the issue, rather than dwelling on it. The constant awareness of your emotions is what will ultimately drive you to succeed.

Not only is it important to be able to recognize your own emotions, but also the emotions of those around you. When you understand how to manage others' emotions in various situations and under various circumstances, you have a better chance of improving the situation and eventually getting the outcome that you desire.

Emotional intelligence can also benefit your health in a big way. Being able to manage your stress levels will lower your blood pressure, decrease your risk of obesity, heart attacks and stroke, and keep your immune system strong. In addition to your physical health, you will feel stronger mentally, which is imperative when living a successful life.

Stress and anxiety can make you feel depressed, lonely, and worrisome. Learning to maintain your composure and transfer your emotional energy into something more productive will only improve your quality of life.

Give yourself a break. All work and no play is sure to send your stress levels through the roof and will certainly alter the way you react in different scenarios. Take some time out of your busy life to collect your thoughts and enjoy yourself. You are entitled to a vacation from time to time. Keeping a level head at all times is crucial in order to be successful. After all, emotional intelligence is linked to performance, which means the higher your emotional intelligence is, the better you will perform.

You are more likely to succeed in life if you have a strong grasp on your emotions and know how to use them effectively. Responding to others' concerns and problems, conflict resolution, and simply being aware of your emotions and your surroundings are tools for leadership, customer service, and overall success.

There is a difference between emotional intelligence and IQ. In fact, they are essentially unrelated and very different. Your IQ measures your ability to learn and your cognitive intelligence. It also stays the same throughout your life. Emotional intelligence is how well you can manage and control your emotions. It can be developed at any age and can become stronger with practice. A person with a high IQ is not necessarily emotionally intelligent.

Emotional intelligence does not appear more prominently in one gender over the other. Some people believe that women tend to have stronger emotional intelligence than men, but they do not. Women do, however, handle their emotions differently. Women are more likely to be self-aware of their own emotions and are also more empathetic when it comes to managing others' emotions. Men tend to be more upbeat, confident and able to deal with stress better. Slight differences aside, neither sex is more competent than the other when it comes to emotional intelligence. In the end, they end up balancing each other out.

People who are in touch with their emotions are more likely to thrive in a managerial or leadership position than those who are not. Employees look to them for guidance and the ability to make level-headed decisions in problematic situations. Having good time-management, social skills, and excellent self-esteem are key qualities to have when in a leadership position. It is also imperative that you do not let your emotions and surroundings define and affect who you are as a person.

In addition to management, emotional intelligence will benefit you in any professional position. Employers will appreciate your open and level mind, your ability to be a team player, and your problem solving skills. Employers also like to hire people with an upbeat and confident personality who can interact well with their clients and their co-workers.

By having strong emotional intelligence, you will thrive more in your personal life as well. You will be able to understand and meet the needs of your partner in your romantic relationship. Your friendships and social skills will improve. You will be able to resolve problematic situations that pop up in your life in a less stressful and more efficient way. You'll notice your stress levels become significantly lower and that you develope a more positive outlook on life.

You will want to succeed and will want others to succeed as well. By looking inward, and discovering how to control your emotions, you will be improving your quality of life. Remaining positive through the trials and errors of mastering your emotional intelligence is what will ultimately get you through it. You will begin to recognize positive changes in your personal and professional relationships which will motivate you to continue to learn how to control and express your emotions in every situation.

Chapter 2: 3 EQ Models Every Business Leader Needs to Know

"Effective Leaders are alike in one crucial way: they all have a high degree of emotional intelligence." – Daniel Goleman

As we open the door to the notion of emotional intelligence, we find that, as a leader, we are forced not only to deal with a diverse group of people daily but also continuously confront the same questions. How do we make the right decision? How do we motivate our team? How do we do things better?

The core of everything, however, is the same: a willingness to changes and adapt to suit the needs of the workforce and the company. We will soon learn that if we can properly balance and redirect the way we lead.

Once you begin to understand the importance of emotion and emotional intelligence, you will automatically realize that you are in need of a solid theoretical base from which you can work forward – this theoretical base is henceforth provided in the form of the three most important models of emotional intelligence produced by modern research.

These three models once properly understood and instilled can and will act as the gravitational center of all your leadership decisions, and will act as an anchor and a tool to help you simplify and tackle any upcoming and current problem. It is, in other words, your light at the end of the tunnel, not just a beacon of hope, but also a guide to lead you forward.

Now, are you ready to brush up on your theory?

Mixed Model Intelligence

"When your intuition is highly developed, you don't have to work to turn it on. It stays on; it flows. It becomes part of the way your heart and senses relate to every experience and circumstance." – Robert Cooper

The good news is, unlike IQ, which is mostly built in and fixated after our teen years, our EQ is learned and can be learned at any age. In fact, there are five specific components of emotional intelligence that help buoy your ability to function with better emotional stability, which is covered in the David Goleman model of EQ, a.k.a. the Mixed Model.

Self-Awareness

The development of self-awareness as a business leader is critical. As a business leader, after all, you need to be aware of your own moods and emotions so that you can also follow and anticipate how they will impact others. It is also important because self-awareness allows you to understand what motivates you as an individual. The more in tune you are with your personal strengths, weaknesses, interests, and disinterests, the better you will be able to control and influence your own actions.

Self-awareness allows a person to have a strong sense of self-worth as well. This is super important as it lets you identify your own strengths and teaches you how to accept criticism, which is a critical part of human development. Such a need intensifies when you become a business leader because the more you develop self-awareness, the more your organization can grow under your leadership.

Sample Scenario

As a leader, it is important that you understand what impact you have on the people you are leading. Imagine for a minute that Lord Voldemort decides to have a board meeting with all of his Death Eaters to gain their opinions on how he should treat Harry Potter, who happens to be their current prisoner. Given the reputation that Voldemort has forged, it is unlikely for his followers to tell him what they genuinely think he should do. Due to his fearsome nature, it is more possible for him to receive lip service.

Now, imagine that you are the CEO of MAC, and you have developed a tendency to lash out at the bearers of bad news, often by firing or demoting them. You have recently assembled a board meeting to ask your senior executives how a lipstick that you have personally been seeking to produce may fare on the global market. How likely is it for your senior managers to speak up?

A good leader understands not just what other people are prone to do but how they behave and impact others as well.

Self-Control

Self-control is another extremely important competency. Unlike self-awareness that focuses on the understanding of the self, self-control concentrates on the ability to conform and redirect actions or reactions. This way, the things that we do are not impulsive. Self-control works to actively increase the process of rational thinking under pressure and is meant to encourage and boost productive actions.

Sample Scenario

Let's go back to the Lord Voldemort scenario that we have just dealt with. Like Lord Voldemort, you have been made aware that your tendency to lash out and use Avada Kedavra on all of your opinionated Death Eaters has somewhat turned you into a tyrant. You now have two options: acknowledge and disregard this information or act on it. The thing is, emotionally stable and intelligent individuals would choose to do the latter. As such, the Mixed Model seeks to measure one's ability to impose self-control to see how emotionally intelligent a person is.

Now, let's take a look at the MAC scenario again. Lack of self-control means that even though you are aware that your actions as a CEO cause you to lose valid opposition or something as simple as a second opinion, which, in turn, makes your company garner unnecessary and preventable losses. Neither of these things add up to you being a smart or great leader. In contrast, if you taught yourself how to be more accepting of changes, you would be able to not just adjust your product but also come off as more approachable and less of a tyrant. In the end, you can't just always be right, because no one ever is. As a leader, your job is to be right for the company, even at the cost of your own pride or emotions, and that is where self-control comes in.

Motivation

It is extremely important to keep in mind that one's ability and will to work do not merely depend on the logical factors that generally govern work-life balance, such as monetary gain or professional advancement. There are many times in which a person's desire to work comes from something more basic like their passion or determination to do well and succeed in life. And these factors, when combined together, are what we often call as motivation. The thing is, it is more than just drive. It is the force that allows someone to easily overcome the obstacles that they will undoubtedly face as they continue to pursue their goals. That is exactly why any good leader needs to have a strong grasp of what motivates their employees and how to increase those motivational levels best.

Why?

While being aware of how you impact your employees is great, so is being able to control your own emotions. Nevertheless, what's genuinely important is having the ability to handle your employee's emotions, which is basically what motivation does.

Sample Scenario

Once upon a time, Walt Disney didn't have enough money to make movies. So, he went to his brother, but then he got turned down. Walt went to a man named Mike Vance and asked him to get more money out of Disneyland. Mr. Vance did it by putting together a team of seven people, who recommended that they should open the park on Mondays and Tuesdays, which were holidays at the time while providing a corporate discount. The idea was a massive hit. As a thank you, Walt Disney personally sent over Mickey Mouse to each of the seven members with an envelope containing 100 shares of Disney stock, $25,000, and a handwritten note that said, "It's fantastic. You're fantastic. Do it again." Now, what do you think happened the next time Walt called them in?

They came in, of course! That is exactly how motivation works. It not only gets the job done but also makes sure it keeps on getting done, which is what every great leader should aspire to!

Empathy

Empathy is also very important, particularly for business leaders. It allows a good leader to feel what other people - more importantly, what their co-workers or employees - feel. Even in cases wherein a leader is unable to completely understand others' emotions, the mere establishment of the intent to reach out, understand, and work through these problems is a core skill for any mentor. Especially for people in diverse work cultures, that is such an integral part of today's business world.

Sample Scenario

We've talked about this before, but it is worth repeating that we are no longer dealing with one-dimensional transactional sales anymore. Company sales depend on the experience the consumer is gaining and not on the simple product that is being purchased these days. As such, it is crucial for companies to learn how to sell their image, which - surprise, surprise - is so much easier to do when the business comes off as nice. Think of Walgreen's for a minute. The company, thanks to its then-VP Randy Lewis, began a disability inclusion program, which showed significant business gains after a year. Turns out, when a company comes off as empathetic, the consumers tend to like it a little bit more. Who knew?!

Social Skill

Finally, we find ourselves dealing with social skill. Despite being able to empathize, understand, and even control our own emotions, it is impossible to be a good business leader if one cannot demonstrate strong and consistent ability to deal with conflict situations and manage mutually beneficial relationships. This skill to be whoever their consumer and employees need them to be is always common in every great leader.

A person manages to do that by obtaining and maintaining a high degree of emotional intelligence, of course!

Sample Scenario

Imagine that you are the CEO of a Fortune 500 company but are unfortunately extremely awkward. Not only do you have a hard time keeping up with your peers; you also have a tendency to offend and cause problems among your allies. You will basically end up being the Donald Trump of the business world. Aside from ruining the company's image, you will also come off as incompetent and destructive. None of your EQ is worth anything if you cannot attend to the situations you are faced with in a manner that is appropriate. Remember, in order to rule the roost, you need to be a rooster first!

Emotional Intelligence Trait Model

"Before you can lead others, before you can help others, you have to discover yourself." – Joe Jaworski

The final model that we'll be dealing with here is the Emotional Intelligence Trait Model, which has been defined by its developer Konstantin Vasily Petrides, as "a constellation of emotional self-perceptions located at the lower levels of personality."[2] This specific model does not merely test one's perception of their own emotions, but it does so in a manner that allows self-assessment to help build the EQ framework. It has often been criticized for its vulnerability to result in manipulation. For instance, if a person decides to answer dishonestly, their EQ would theoretically be scored incorrectly; however, the model itself has been known to reject such implications. A basic Trait Model EQ test imposed on an adult would consist of the measure of 15 major points.

Adaptability

Adaptability is an individual's emotional intelligence trait that is considered to indicate his or her flexibility. It refers to how rigid they are in their own thought pattern, as well as how capable they are of adapting to newfound situations or conditions. Adaptability is a key component of emotional intelligence, considering the only way to bolster teamwork is by putting together a cohesive team and showing a willingness to change their ways, which is something that any good leader should be on the lookout for.

Assertiveness

Next up is assertiveness. It is a sociability trait that determines the individual's ability to stand up for the rights that they have inherited or gained, as well as communicate their feelings or opinions in a frank and forthright way. The higher the assertiveness of an individual is, the more emotionally intelligent they are considered to be. After all, the trait is indicative of clarity and consistency of mind.

Emotional Expression

Emotional expression is a similarly important trait. Unlike assertiveness, however, emotional expression is an emotionality trait that determines how capable a person is at communicating their thoughts and feelings to other people. The higher a person scores on their emotional expression, the more in tune they are with their emotionality and personal views. This serves as an indicator of high emotional intelligence.

Emotional Management

Another sociability trait is emotional management. This is thought to measure how well an individual can use their other sociability skills, such as assertiveness, to control and influence other people, especially their thoughts and feelings. The more adept a person is at managing or controlling others' emotions, the higher their emotional intelligence score is, considering the entire objective of emotional intelligence is to be able to exert some sort of control over other people through emotional manipulation.

Emotional Perception

Unlike emotional management, though, emotional perception centers more around the emotionality factor and is used to check how comprehensive one's understanding is of their own feelings, as well as the others'. It is another extremely important factor since most actions are undertaken due to the individuals' understanding of the emotional state of the other person or even themselves.

Emotional Regulation

Emotional regulation, on the other hand, falls under the category of self-control and is a trait that assesses how capable the individual is when it comes to not only influencing but completely controlling and regulating how people feel regularly. The better a person is at handling their own emotions, the better and more balanced their decisions will be, and the more likely it is for these decisions to be good. As such, emotional regulation is another key factor measured.

Impulsiveness

Another self-control variety that trait models measure is the scale of impulsiveness that is displayed by individuals. Unlike the other sectors in this book, the lower the impulsiveness levels a person shows, the higher their emotional intelligence is deemed to be. The reason is that being impulsive is the exact opposite of acting with emotional intelligence. In truth, it has a tendency to destabilize any decision because it is usually a not-well-thought-out reaction.

Relationships

Another emotionality-based trait is relationships. A critical part of measuring emotional intelligence is weighing a subject's ability to not only perceive or act on but also fully function in an emotionally balanced manner to maintain personal relationships that are meaningful and fulfilling. Think of Sheldon Cooper's ability to keep friendships and relationships as opposed to a normal person - that is what you're trying to avoid. Sheldon from the first season of Big Bang Theory is not very high on the EQ scale, and maintaining personal relationships is challenging for him. His other friends like Penny may not have a high IQ level, but they are quite capable in terms of EQ maintenance.

Self-Esteem

How a person views himself or herself is also an important part of emotional intelligence. You should keep in mind, however, that the trait test is not a simple case of high means good or low equates bad in terms of its scoring. On the contrary, each score is contextually based. As it involves self-assessment, it is based more on the perceptions that someone has of himself or herself instead of the actual measure of competencies or skills that the individuals hold. Nevertheless, positive well-being is determined by higher levels of self-esteem, among other factors.

Self-Motivation

Self-motivation is one of the auxiliary facets of the test that is used to assess how driven an individual perceives themselves to be and how likely they are to either succeed or persist in their attempts to achieve a goal despite the situation at hand. In other words, it seeks to measure how much drive an individual has when it comes to how they approach issues daily.

Self-Awareness

Interestingly, self-awareness, which is a sociability factor, differs from self-esteem and self-motivation, in the sense that it does not measure any positive view that one may have or think they have about themselves. Instead, it seems single-mindedly focused on identifying how accomplished a person is in terms of how they perceive their own social skills and subsequent networking abilities. It matters to keep in mind that awareness does not depend on how good one is about their skills but how well they can realize whatever abilities they have.

Stress Management

Emotional or stress management is another sociability factor and the last of the three used to measure trait EQ. An individual's perception of their ability to withstand and work under stress, as well as their perceived ability to regulate or control the stress levels imposed on them are both identified through stress management.

Trait Empathy

Another emotionality trait measured is empathy. Here, the individual's perception of how far they can commiserate and objectively see the world from the eyes of another person is identified and accounted for.

Trait Happiness

The happiness trait, on the other hand, deals with how a person perceives their ability to be happy, how happy they think they are, and how satisfied they are with their own lives. Hence, the well-being of an individual is judged in part by the happiness trait.

Trait Optimism

The last trait is measured by trait optimism, which, as a rule, checks how likely an individual is to confidently look at the positives - or on the "bright side," as people put it.

With EQ tests measuring different parts and many other factors, it is clear that emotional intelligence plays a critical role in terms of predicting job performance. As such, it has a very specific impact on contextual happenstances. It practically means that there is a positive correlation between the two. Emotional intelligence can be used to approach organizational behavior as a tool, which will not only help explain problems in the workforce but actively and effectively navigate through its waters as well.

Emotional Intelligence Ability

"Perhaps the most irrational assumption we can make is assuming that people should behave rationally and unemotionally." – Dean Tvosjold

The ability model is an EQ model developed by Yale's Peter Salovey and University of New Hampshire's John Mayer. It is based on four individually standing yet interconnected emotion-related abilities. when combined, they can basically measure the level of emotional intelligence that an individual has. These four abilities have been identified and are discussed in detail below.

Emotional Perception

The first and most basic ability is perception. In order to accurately master and apply emotions and emotional intelligence, one must first be able to not only understand the verbal emotional cues provided but also accurately identify the non-verbal cues that workers and peers use in their regular interactions. Non-verbal cues include body language, facial expression, tone, vocabulary, and even contextual behavior or omission of an act. To become a good leader, you need to pick up these cues and identify them masterfully.

Sample Scenario

Jon Snow is a great leader. When he's told about how his people are feeling and what goes on around him, he can make the right decision and always put them first. He is also a righteous ruler who never places his own personal wants or desires above the needs and rights of the people he is in charge of.

The only problem with Jon Snow is that he "knows nothing." Meaning to say, as a leader, he lacks the ability to perceive or identify the thoughts and needs of the individuals he serves. He is also unable to understand the motives or intentions of the people he surrounds himself with unless he is specifically told in some overt way about, say, the burning down a city. As such, Jon's ability to lead is entirely dependent on the information he receives.

Question: Can you still say that Jon is a great leader?

Answer: No. In order to be one, Jon should be able to identify and then assess the threats and possibilities that surround him. While he is capable of making the right decision, he can only do that when he is spoon-fed with information, which, in reality, is not something that is always going to happen. Due to his inability to accurately perceive the thoughts and emotional triggers of the people he is supposed to lead, therefore, Jon Snow is effectively blinded by ill-meaning folks and rendered unable to become an effective leader.

Use of Emotion

The second most important ability according to the ability model is the capacity to control and use one's own emotions, as well as the emotions of other people, to your advantage. It is an undisputed fact that feelings play a major role in the decision-making process. We have already highlighted how emotions can even influence logical decisions and lead to emotion-based ideas and logical fallacies. However, what we haven't really touched upon is the truth that, despite all this, every decision not taken by a robot or AI is still influenced by some degree of emotion. As such, it is critical for a leader to know how to mold and manipulate their feelings to achieve their desired ends. This is particularly vital when a leader is dealing with an issue that needs to be resolved at once.

Sample Scenario

Let's say you are in the middle of negotiating a merger between Microsoft (a company that you lead) and Apple. Apple is represented by a man named Ross Geller, who is the head of its corporate negotiations team. Unfortunately, he is also currently dealing with mental distress because he happens to be going through a bad breakup with Rachel Green, his girlfriend. This woman works for your company as the chief of corporate strategy, and so she has to represent Microsoft in the current dealings. Inexplicably, the merger keeps on facing irrational obstacles that are usually generated by Mr. Geller every time he comes across a point being put forward by Ms. Green.

Because you are unable to understand how to use emotions, you don't understand why Mr. Geller can't seem to come to a rational compromise.

Question: Are you being a good leader?

Answer: No. Although the idea of Mr. Geller representing Apple and Ms. Green being in attendance for Microsoft seems good at first, and while removing either of them from the negotiations can be unfair because they are both entitled to be in the meeting for their respective companies due to the posts that they hold, you, as a leader, seem to be missing the point entirely. Your job is not only to cater to logic but also usher in an effective and positive progression. Because of the emotional baggage that both parties hold on to, it is irrational to expect them to behave reasonably. Therefore, you should know better than to expect them to be able to come to an amicable settlement.

Instead, if you send other members on your team who are equally or adequately equipped to go to the meeting, you will be using your EQ to navigate the current situation in a manner the is beneficial to you and your company. This is the mark of good leadership. Alternatively, if you want to stall the deal because you are also in talks with Yahoo! for a similar merger, you may continue to have Mr. Geller and Ms. Green as the representatives of their respective companies. Doing so can buy you some time and allow you to see how the second option pans out.

Understanding Emotions

Another important part of EQ is the ability to properly comprehend the depth and implications of emotion. Now, unlike what most people seem to think, identifying an emotion is not always enough. Furthermore, it is hard to navigate through it without understanding its root and effects first. For instance, if you were dealing with an individual who happened to be angry, your first question as a leader should be "Why?" By unmasking the reasoning that the individual is using, whether or not you agree with it, you are also giving yourself insight into the possible future actions that he or she may take. When it comes to anger, after all, a possible future action can be seeking revenge, attacking, or retreating fearfully. As a leader, you need to have that insight into all of your employees and other people you interact with. Remember, knowledge is power, and EQ is emotional knowledge at its peak.

Question: How can understanding emotions differ from emotional navigation? How does it change the way you approach the workforce?

Answer: Imagine yourself as Dany Targarean, the CEO of Unsullied, Inc. As such, you have been put in charge of a failing company called Westeroes, which just declared bankruptcy last week. Now, you have decided to employ Ms. Cersai Lannister, former CEO of Westeroes, as the CFO of your company, even though she holds a major grudge against you for taking over and blames you and Unsullied Inc. for the financial ruin of Westeroes. As a CEO, have you made the best possible decision by putting Ms. Lannister in charge of its financial future?

No! Of course not. While it is entirely likely that you were attempting a gesture of good faith or that Ms. Lannister was Sheldon Cooper's counterpart in the world of financing, the fact remains that Ms. Lannister bears a grudge towards you and your company for some reason, logical or not. Hence, she is unlikely to want the best for the business and may genuinely wish to see its financial downfall. If you cannot spot an emotionally vulnerable employee, it entails that you are a liability to your own company as well.

Managing Emotions

This brings us to the final emotional competency measured by the ability model: the management of emotions. Managing emotions deals with three main factors - is the person in question being able to adequately take into account the emotions that they are perceiving? If they are, then are they comprehensively using those emotions to control the root cause and reactive elements in question.

Chapter 3: Understanding Intelligence

The Changing Face of the Intelligent

The significance of understanding intelligence is incontestable. For many years, psychologists have been trying to understand, categorize and define human intelligence. Studies and researches have been made to fathom the nature of intelligence and most of the time these works measure intelligence using IQ.

Psychologists recognized, since the eighteenth century, that the mind consists of a three-part division. These parts include cognitive, effect and the motivation (or cognition). The cognitive part is the one responsible for memory, reasoning, abstract thought and judgment. For several years psychologists and other experts usually use the word intelligence to characterize how well this cognitive part of the mind functions (Mayer, 1997).

There are several theories, whether they are hoary or contemporary, that are elucidating the idea of having more than one aspect or type of intelligence and this has been recognized in the field of psychology for many years. Nevertheless, a good measure of one's cognitive ability suffices the broad notion of intelligence for the past years. Indeed, cognitive intelligence is the kind of intelligence most people know and understand.

This traditional view of intelligence has been challenged and is still being challenged at present. The emerging idea, especially in the contemporary, of broadening the understanding of intelligence paved way to the changing face of who and what can be considered intelligent.

Measuring intelligence using only the cognitive part of the human mind is now seen to be insufficient to understand the full potential of human intelligence. High scores in tests measuring memory, reasoning and logic, mathematical skills, and the like are no longer the best indicators of actual performances.

Nature of Intelligence

Intelligence is a commonly-used word; nonetheless, it does not entail that people have a thorough understanding of what the word really means. A conceptual definition of intelligence is the ability to learn from experience, solve problems and use knowledge to adapt in a specific environment. This definition is said to be applicable across cultures. Indeed, individuals differ in their ability to understand complex ideas to successfully adapt in a particular environment or to overcome obstacles. The differences are undeniable and most of the time they are taken into consideration when it comes to attempts in understanding the concept of intelligence holistically. Individual differences are substantial yet inconsistent at times. How a person responds "intellectually" will differ on varying circumstances and in different realms, as they can be observed and judged according to different criteria.

Up until now, there are still unanswered questions surrounding the concept of intelligence. Several conceptualizations and attempts to map out the entirety of intelligence have surfaced through time yet none command a universal acquiescence. Despite the existence of gray areas, still it can be said that there exists a considerable amount of clarity achieved by years and years of studies and researches in some areas.

Intelligence: Ability or Abilities?

Charles Spearman (1863-1945) pioneered the notion of **general intelligence.** This **general intelligence,** as Spearman theorized, is linked to several clusters that can be analyzed by using factor analysis. The studies conducted by Spearman revealed that regardless of the domain of a mental test, the scores tend to load on one major factor, a common pool of mental energy, which he labeled as the **g** or the general factor (Neisser, 1996).

The idea of having a single scale of general intelligence was directly opposed by several other psychologists who stand by the notion of multiple mental abilities. L.L. Thurstone, for instance, identified seven clusters of primary mental abilities, which includes the following: inductive reasoning, memory, numerical ability, perceptual speed, spatial ability, verbal comprehension and word fluency. Some contemporary psychologists agreed with this idea of multiple forms of intelligence. Howard Gardner, in his book Frames of Mind (1983), identified eight types of intelligences including: bodily-kinesthetic, intrapersonal, interpersonal, linguistic, logical-mathematical, musical, naturalistic and spatial. Gardner pointed out that the conception of intelligence must not be limited to studies and works with "normal" people. By looking at different cases of people who are "special" or gifted, people who suffered selective brain damage, people with abilities valued by their own culture and the like, Gardner was able to widen the horizon of his understanding and conceptualization of intelligence. He even carried the speculation of a ninth form of intelligence he named **existential**, which he described as the ability to think about existence, life and death (Neisser, 1996).

Robert Sternberg is another contemporary theorist, who agreed with Gardner with his conception of multiple intelligences. However, Sternberg proposes only three fundamental aspects of intelligence, which includes analytic, creative and practical. Analytic intelligence pertains to one's ability to acquire and store information. This intelligence is what a typical intelligence test is measuring. Creative intelligence, as characterized by Sternberg, is the person's ability to think originally. This intelligence talks about the person's ability to adapt to novel situations (Neisser, 1996).

The New Face of Intelligence

The Significance of Emotional Intelligence

For several years, human intelligence was measured using the IQ yard stick. How well one scores in verbal IQ tests (information comprehension, vocabulary, similarities, digit span and the like) and performance IQ tests (object assembly, digit symbol, picture completion, picture arrangement, block design), was generally used to predict one's success and failure odds. Nevertheless, with the growing numbers of research showing that there is more to intelligence than what cognitive abilities could offer; more and more companies and establishments are now considering looking at a better yardstick to assess intelligence among people, that is, emotional intelligence.

Emotional Intelligence: What Really Is It?

Another form of intelligence, called emotional intelligence, is now gaining considerable attention in various journals, books and magazines. Studies and researches about this intelligence are now continuously growing in numbers. Emotional intelligence, just like any other types of intelligence, is not easy to define. Although there are several authors talking about emotional intelligence, particularly nowadays, there is still no universal definition existing until now.

A broad definition of emotional intelligence states that it is the one responsible for personal, emotional, survival and social dimensions of intelligence. These functions are said to be more important than cognitive aspects of intelligence in day-to-day functioning. Moreover, emotional intelligence is associated with understanding oneself and others, adapting to the immediate surroundings and relating to others to successfully address the demands of the environment.

Emotional intelligence is not really a recent discovery. It has been known in the field for a relatively long time. It is just now that people began to recognize the big role it plays in the entirety of human intelligence.

In 1940, David Wechsler pioneered the study about emotional intelligence. He called it the "non intellective aspect of general intelligence." According to Wechsler, non intellective factors, which include affect and conative abilities, are not just admissible but are necessary factors of general intelligence. Hence, to fully understand or measure total intelligence, one must assess non intellective factors as well (Grayson).

Following Wechsler's proposition, Leeper, in 1948, stated that "emotional thought" is part of logical thought and intelligence in general. These early recognitions of the importance of emotional intelligence have been succeeded by psychologists of the contemporary milieu. Howard Gardner's theory of multiple intelligences, for instance, included emotional or personal dimension in the form of interpersonal and intrapersonal skills. Other psychologists like Peter Salovey and John Mayer devoted their research to understanding the emotional aspect of intelligence. Their works are concentrating on six components of emotional intelligence, which include the following: assertiveness, empathy, emotional self-awareness, interpersonal relationship, impulse control and stress tolerance (Grayson).

There is a plethora of definitions offered to explain what emotional intelligence is. With the absence of a generic conceptualization, one must start with exploring and understanding the relationship of the two big terms, **emotion** and **intelligence,** to come up with a relatively enlightened idea of what emotional intelligence really is. Emotional intelligence, therefore, can best be described by the following words: "the ability to perceive emotions, to access and generate emotions so as to assist thought, to understand emotions and emotional knowledge and to reflectively regulate emotions so as to promote emotional and intellectual growth" (Mayer, 1997).

The definition provided above is among the best descriptions appropriated for the concept of emotional intelligence. What made it more appealing than others is its encompassing conceptualization of how emotion and intelligence are related. The definition was able to intertwine the notions that one thinks intelligently about emotions and emotions make thinking more intelligent.

As mentioned earlier, emotional intelligence is deemed more necessary in the everyday experience than the cognitive aspect of intelligence. For instance, reasoning that takes emotions into consideration (which is a part of emotional intelligence) is usually present in a person's everyday life. Dealing with other people or socializing and self-awareness are common grounds identifying how well one can manage his/her everyday experience. Responding in a specific situation by assessing social factors and one's emotional knowledge identifies how one would manage surviving his/her immediate environment. All of these factors are aspects of emotional intelligence and these are the reasons why more attention has now been given to studying emotional intelligence as a key factor in determining a person's ability to be successful in life.

Indeed, more and more studies show support that emotional intelligence can be a more accurate indicator of a person's behavior and performance. This aspect of intelligence can help predict success primarily because it reflects how a person would utilize knowledge to his/her immediate situation. Getting along with the world is a key factor for one to be successful in life, and that is exactly what emotional intelligence of a person could identify. With these reasons some industries are now giving more priority to emotional intelligence than the traditional cognitive aspect.

Redefining the "Smart"

Neither having outstanding scholastic achievements nor having memorized every step in the technical know-how by heart and by experience will no longer guarantee a person his/her dream job. With substantial amount of studies valuing the importance of emotional intelligence to job performances, more and more companies are now utilizing EQ tests to applicants in addition to the traditional IQ tests. Some companies are even giving more priority to EQ results than the IQ scores.

The workplace can be the best ground to see how emotional intelligence redefines what it means to be smart. There are just several intertwining relationships that occur in a workplace. A person needs to deal with several others primarily because they are working as one unit. In such situations, being the most cognitively intelligent individual is one thing, but knowing how to effectively deal with people from different walks of life is surely another thing.

The success of a company relies largely on how well-established are the relationships of the working individuals within the firm. This is the reason why most companies are now looking at the emotional aspect of intelligence of applicants and employees in deciding whom to hire or whom to keep and whom to let go. According to studies, EQ predicts higher performance three times better than IQ. Even leadership requires a higher level of emotional intelligence than of the cognitive one. Thus, it is said that the higher the job position, the more emotional intelligence is needed (Goleman, 1998).

Emotional intelligence, however, must not be mistaken as just "being nice." Moreover it does not entail completely surrendering to one's feelings. Emotional intelligence determines a person's potential in learning practical skills that are based on elements that include self-regulation, self-awareness, motivation, empathy and adeptness. These skills, unlike the ones measured by IQ, are said to be uncontrolled by genetics and not learned in traditional academe. Everyone can develop the above-mentioned skills.

The Intelligence of a Social Being

People are social beings. Building relationships with other people is basic to human nature. One cannot just live without forming any kind of connection with the rest of the world. This reality explains why emotional intelligence is important. Emotions have the power to override thoughts and to profoundly influence a person's behavior. Therefore knowing and understanding emotions of the self and others can greatly contribute to building a good and healthy relationship with the rest of the world.

The success in life can be largely attributed to how one handles webbed relationships in certain circumstances. How a person responds to dire situations, for instance, cannot be better explained by how good he/she is in written tests in logic, math or vocabulary than by how he/she developed his/her emotional intelligence.

Chapter 4. Leadership, Social Competence and Managing Others' Emotions

Relationship Management

As mentioned in the previous section, social competence can be broken down into two main aspects: social awareness and relationship management. In the previous section, we have defined social awareness and why it is important in improving one's EQ. Now, let us move on to the second aspect of social competence – relationship management.

Relationship management begins with the concept of social awareness. However, in this aspect of social competence, an individual uses social awareness in order to build strong, mutually beneficial, and lasting relationships with other people. This makes sense considering that being attuned to the feelings of others allows an individual to relate better to other people, thereby making it easier to evoke feelings of kinship. In order to improve one's relationship management, there are certain abilities which an individual must develop. These abilities are: influence, leadership, developing others, and communication. Let us go through these abilities one by one.

Influence pertains to the extent by which an individual can persuade others to do things or see things from a different perspective. Influential people are able to gain the support of others and are generally perceived as trustworthy. Leadership pertains to the ability to prompt other people to follow one's lead. Individuals with strong leadership skills lead by example and are able to inspire other people to pursue certain goals or achieve a vision. Developing others pertains to the ability to be attuned to the skills and growth potential of other people, and providing others with an avenue for improving themselves. Finally, communication pertains to the ability to effectively put one's feelings into words and other non-verbal cues, thereby facilitating the exchange of information between individuals. People with good communication skills are better able to relate with others since they can easily articulate their feelings.

Relationship management is important in maintaining high EQ because individuals do not exist in a vacuum. As such, one must be able to understand emotions not only in the context of one's self, but also as related to other people. Managing relationships effectively gives one the opportunity to improve one's self in relation to, and with the help of, other people. Effective relationship management also prompts an individual to hold his own emotions in check in relation to the people around him. Individuals with great relationship management skills are well-adjusted, open to change, and have better and stronger support systems than those who do not.

Understanding Your Impact On Others

If one is to build healthy and meaningful relationships with other people, it is necessary to first have a good understanding of how one impacts others. The adage "no man is an island" might be a cliché, but it is quite true. Realizing that one's actions has repercussions to the people around them prompts an individual to be more mindful of his actions and behaviors. That said, if you are aiming to be more emotionally intelligent, then you should understand how you impact the feelings of the people around you.

Impacting the emotions of the people around you is a two-step process. First, you need to be confident in your ability to influence other people. Second, you need to know how to positively impact the emotions of others. Let us discuss the first step.

We all have an innate ability to affect the feelings of the people around us, whether or not we realize it. What spells the difference between an emotionally intelligent person and your average Joe is the confidence in doing so. If you want to have a positive impact on others, you first have to realize that you are capable of doing so. Note, however, that there is often a fine line between confidence and arrogance. It is one thing to know that you can affect the people around you; it is another to think that the world revolves around you. Remember that you want to impact other people positively, so you have to be wary of how you present yourself to the people around you.

Second, it is necessary for you to know how exactly you can affect the feelings of the people around you positively. This entails being attentive to the needs and wants of others. Note that every individual has different emotional needs and responds differently to various factors. Thus, if you want to uplift the people around you, you should learn how to pay attention to their emotions and you should figure out which actions or behaviors they respond positively to. Being able to positively impact the emotions of others will not only make you well-liked, it will also make you feel better about yourself. The good thing about positivity is that it circles around. Thus, if you make someone feel good about themselves, they are also more likely to respond positively to you, thereby making you feel good in the process as well.

Being Assertive

Another notable characteristic of emotionally intelligent people is assertiveness. Unfortunately, being assertive can often be confused with being aggressive. Hence, it is necessary to differentiate between assertiveness and aggressiveness.

Simply speaking, assertive people are not afraid of voicing out their opinions and taking a stand, but remain mindful and respectful of the people around them in doing so. Meanwhile, aggressive people tend to air their opinions by talking over other people, ignoring them, or even attacking them. That said, while assertive individuals earn the respect of their colleagues and are often lauded for their honesty, aggressive people tend to foster ill will and antagonistic attitudes. In terms of leadership, people are more likely to willingly heed the call and advice of someone who is assertive as compared to someone who is aggressive.

To illustrate, let us take Mary and Joan. Say they are both in a meeting and, due to differences in opinion among the members of the team, the team cannot seem to agree on which course of action to take. Both Mary and Joan have something to say, but they say it differently. Mary is aggressive, so she tries to get people to listen to her views by attacking the other members of the team, calling them "unimpressive" or "not bright enough to give suggestions". In reality, Mary is extremely good at what she does, but the importance of her suggestions is diminished by the harshness in which she delivers them.

Meanwhile, Joan is assertive. She is polite and waits for her turn to speak. She addresses the points made by her colleagues, all the while incorporating her own. At the end of the meeting, the team puts to a vote which suggestion to actually take. Everyone votes for Joan's even if both hers and Mary's are viable options. The reason Joan was heard out? She takes a stand but remains respectful of the people around her.

There are a lot of situations wherein assertiveness can really come handy. The obvious example is when you want your views to be heard, but it is equally important in saying no, in standing up for yourself, or even in holding on to your convictions. Being assertive will allow you to actively choose options which are good for you, without having to sacrifice the emotional well-being of the people around you. Hence, assertiveness is a lesson on confidence as much as it is a lesson on self-control.

You are a Natural Born Leader

Another important facet of emotional intelligence is good leadership. In fact, people with high EQ tend to be great leaders with substantial followings. So what makes a great leader? What is the importance of being one?

A great leader is one who leads by example, someone who can motivate the people around them into action. While there are individuals who are natural born leaders and are simply inherently good with people, leadership skills can be developed through practice and mindfulness of one's presentation to others. Hence, if you want to improve your leadership skills, then you need to know first what makes a good leader.

Good leaders are not infallible individuals. Quite the contrary, good leaders are those who have a good understanding of their own strengths and weaknesses. That said, they are able to maximize their strengths while, at the same time, delegating tasks which they cannot perform themselves due to their weaknesses. Awareness of their weaknesses makes good leaders humble while at the same time, accessible insofar as their subordinates are concerned. Also, by delegating tasks to others, they are able to foster a sense of involvement and camaraderie which facilitates the building of a meaningful relationship.

That said, good leaders must know where their core competencies lie. Having leadership skills does not mean doing all the work yourself. Rather, it entails knowing which particular things you can do well and which ones to outsource to other people. As such, individuals who take on too much responsibility and end up spreading themselves to thin are rarely considered great leaders. On the contrary, those who know what they can do and what they do well tend to be more effective in taking up leadership positions, especially since they get to concentrate on various aspects of whatever project they are in charge of.

Being a good leader also entails having a solid character and a clear sense of what you are and what you want to be. Note that people tend to look up to leaders, so there is as much praise as there is pressure and scrutiny. Despite the pressure, however, taking up leadership positions and handling them well is good training in terms of improving one's EQ since you get to meet a lot of people, meet with them, and influence others, all the while learning how to get a better hold of your emotions and how to project yourself properly.

Social Awareness and Social Competence

Social awareness and social competence are two integral aspects of emotional intelligence. Hence, increasing one's EQ also entails mastery of these two factors. Social awareness and social competence are two interrelated concepts. More specifically, social awareness is a facet of social competence, which involves various skills. In order to better understand social awareness and social competence, it is best to define them side by side.

As previously mentioned, social competence is the umbrella term under which several capabilities fall under. To be more specific, social competence is composed of two main parts: social awareness (which we will be discussing in this section) and relationship management (which we will be expounding on in the next section). Hence, social competence refers to how an individual fares in social settings in terms of understanding social cues on the one hand and relating to others on the other.

The first aspect of social competence is social awareness. Social awareness refers to the ability to pick up and understand the emotions of other people. Social awareness can further be broken down to several subskills, i.e., empathy, organizational awareness, and service orientation. Empathy pertains to the ability to not only understand another person's feelings, but to actually re-experience them. It is the ability to put one's self in the shoes of another so to speak. Organizational awareness pertains to the ability to read and understand not only the emotions of a certain group, but also their political realities. Finally, service orientation refers to the ability to put empathy into action and help others in their respective quests for personal development.

Social competence and social awareness are both important in developing one's emotional intelligence because it helps an individual become more attuned to the emotions of the people around them. In order to gain a certain level of social awareness, one must first be self-aware. Then and only then can an individual be able to pick up nuances as regards emotions and as regards expression of the same. Without social competence in general and social awareness in particular, an individual will not be able to relate to the people around them, thereby hindering the formation of meaningful relationships which can greatly contribute to one's emotional well-being. That said, for one to be truly emotionally intelligent, it is not only necessary that they be in touch with their emotions, but they must also be in touch with the emotions of other people. Especially the ones around them.

Building Healthy Relationships

High EQ is not just about building a healthy relationship with one's self, but also about building healthy relationships with other people. Note that we are not talking about building relationships in general but, instead, we are specifically striving for healthy ones. This brings us to the question: what are the hallmarks of healthy relationships?

In order to get started on building healthy and meaningful relationships, it is important to know first what makes a healthy relationship. The following are indicative of healthy relationships, regardless of the nature of the same:

- Mutual respect, especially in terms of values and personal boundaries.

- Trust. Misunderstandings are normal parts of any relationship, so it is necessary for both parties to give the other the benefit of the doubt.

- Honesty as regards feelings, feedbacks, expectations, and even criticisms.

- Ability to compromise, especially with regard to deeply-held beliefs and convictions.

- Respect for differences and individuality. A healthy relationship should not make one party mimic the other. Instead, individuality should be fostered within the context of a supportive relationship.

- Open communication. A healthy relationship should be a venue in which both parties feel safe to air their concerns and feel free to reach out to the other in order to settle differences.

- Ability to control outbursts of emotions. Setbacks cannot be avoided. Hence, it is necessary for both parties to learn how to manage strong emotions like anger in order to keep themselves from unwittingly hurting the other.

These seven hallmarks of a healthy relationship apply in various social contexts – ranging from the professional to the romantic. Striving to incorporate all seven will ensure that the relationship is beneficial to the individual's well-being.

Having healthy relationships provides an individual with a safe space and a viable support system. As such, it is necessary to learn how to build healthy relationships if one wants to be more attuned to the feelings of others, as well as learn more about themselves. Building meaningful connections allow an individual to broaden their horizons and explore differing viewpoints which can greatly contribute to personal growth. In addition, forming a close personal bond with others provides an individual with means by which they can further improve both social awareness and relationship management. By building healthy relationships, one gets to experience positive reinforcement and is provided with an opportunity to correct possibly unhealthy behavior or practices.

Developing Empathy

Simply speaking, empathy refers to the ability to understand the feelings of other people in such a way that lets the empathic individual to share and re-experience the feelings and experiences of another. That said, empathy is a step further than sympathy, which is simply the ability to care for the feelings of others. To illustrate, let us take a group of friends: Anne, Mary, and Joan. Let us say that Anne suddenly lost both of her parents to an accident. Mary sympathizes with Anne and understands how terrible the former is feeling. She understands that Anne is heartbroken and shocked, so she is concerned with Anne's well-being. Despite her feelings of sympathy, however, she remains at a loss as to what she can say or offer to Anne given the magnitude of the latter's predicament. On the other hand, Joan empathizes with Anne. Joan has not gone through what Anne is going through, but she feels her pain nonetheless. Not only does Joan fully understand what Anne is presently experiencing, she relates to that pain as well. That said, Joan is able to offer words of consolation that are more heart-felt. Joan knows exactly what to say to Anne to let her know that she is not alone, but without invalidating Anne's feelings.

Developing empathy entails putting oneself in someone else's shoes. Hence, an individual does not remain a mere passive observer but, instead, takes an active part in another person's experiences. That said, in order to develop empathy, one must forego any preconceived notions and approach others with a certain sense of curiosity. By not having assumptions about another person's experiences, an individual is placed in a better position to understand the point of view of other people. In addition to foregoing assumptions, developing empathy also entails focusing on other people. Much of our prejudices stem from us looking inwardly instead of outwardly when relating with other people. Thus, if we are to empathize, it is necessary that we direct our attention to the person we are trying to empathize with – how they are doing and what they are feeling. That said, deeply empathic individuals are those who understand that the circumstances are not about them but about other people, so to speak. Empathy is important in developing EQ because it demands that the individual develop a deep understanding of one's own emotions and use that understanding to better relate to other people.

Chapter 5: How Emotional Intelligence Helps you with Confidence

When we don't have enough emotional intelligence, our self-esteem suffers. We must pause in order to handle what is bothering us so we can learn to become joyful and at peace with ourselves and in life. One of the most important factors of EQ is confidence in yourself. This quality is nearly always there in the people that others respect and admire. People who feel positively toward themselves, free of arrogance, are the people who we consider to have their act figured out.

What does a Healthy Self-Confidence Look Like?

Having self-confidence means having a balanced and positive perspective about who you are and consists of the conviction that you can accomplish whatever you want. When problems pop up, a confident person will continue working to get through the issue, while someone who isn't as confident would probably not persist and may never begin the task to begin with. Getting through setbacks and feeling proud when we have achieved something is an important part of building up your confidence, even when the goals are small to begin with.

Insecurity is something that everyone in this world has struggled with before in their lives. But did you know that becoming more emotionally intelligence can help you build self-esteem? Insecurity comes on as the result of letting insecure, often irrational thoughts take over your mind and get to you. Since emotional intelligence is all about knowing how to manage your thoughts and feelings and still function successfully, this can be a great way to get your confidence growing and to have a healthy self-esteem. Let's look at some of the basics of this concept.

When you Know yourself, You're Comfortable with Who you are:

People who suffer from a lack of confidence often aren't sure who they are. They feel uncertain about their place in life, which makes them afraid to speak up. They constantly fear looking bad in front of others, which makes them act shy.

When you're Comfortable with Yourself, you aren't Insecure:

When you know yourself and are comfortable, you are not insecure around others. When you take the time to develop your emotional intelligence, your confidence will soar. So, how do you do this?

How to Improve your Confidence and EQ:

To begin improving your confidence, you can start by writing out a script of positivity for yourself. This will be a monologue that goes on inside of you to boost your sense of self-esteem. Think carefully about what this statement will say and write it down. Hold onto this and keep it somewhere that you can refer to it throughout the day. This will remind you of your journey to self-confidence. Here is an example of what the statement can look like:

"I respect myself and know that I am here for a reason. I care about being a kind person to others and try my best every day."

Your statement can be as long as you want, but a couple of sentences is a good start. If your statement doesn't perfectly align with who you are at the moment, you can spend your free time coming up with ways to make that a reality for you. If you are having trouble coming up with a mission statement, take some time to write about it and reflect. When you find that your life situation is very different from your statement, it can be difficult to feel truly self-confident.

Arrogance- a Symptom of Low Emotional Intelligence:

Having a low sense of self-confidence will negatively impact your life, but there is another problematic issue that usually comes along with a low EQ and that is arrogance. When someone acts overconfident, they are trying to make up for an inner lack, and this is a destructive quality to have. People who believe that they are better than others and act domineering are just as ineffective as people who have no confidence at all, because this trait leads to resentment and conflict.

When someone doesn't have confidence, they show a few key signs. These are trouble with admitting when they were wrong, the inability to say sorry, being pushy, or bragging to others. Although people who brag may appear confident at a first glance, when someone is truly confident, they don't feel this need because they already know of their worth and don't need to convince other people. When someone is overly concerned about appearing competent to others, they cannot admit when they are wrong, meaning that it's harder to take advice from well-meaning people around us. However, developing a strong EQ involves this step.

Chapter 6: How to Increase Your Self-Awareness

"Know thyself!" –Socrates

How well do you understand your character, emotions, motivations, strengths, and weaknesses? Self-awareness helps us understand what we are and what other people see in us. It also helps determine how similar or different we are from others.

Emotional intelligence promotes self-awareness. Some of the advantages of being self-aware include:

- Finding yourself
- Expressing yourself
- Understanding others
- Practicing empathy
- Having positive relationships
- Having clarity of mind

You get to develop your self-awareness through introspection. This is all about questioning your motivations – why you act or think in a certain way. Some of the questions you may ask yourself include:

- Why do you value certain things?
- Are you living responsibly?
- Are you moral or immoral?
- Why do you love certain things/people?
- Why do you hate certain things/people?

Here are some of the tips for increasing your self-awareness:

Know your strengths and weakness

Having a clear understanding of areas that you're weak and strong in is a great step towards increasing your self-awareness. This is important because after knowing your strengths, you can seek more ways to capitalize on it. On the other hand, knowing your weaknesses can encourage you to do something about it. For instance, if you have a weakness for binge eating, and it is showing in your waistline, it may affect your self-image. And so, through introspection, you might be able to identify the link between your binge eating and your self-esteem issues and perhaps cut out the binge eating and turn to healthy meals and workouts to get the body that you want. Finding out your weaknesses and strengths is a continuous process.

Try new things

When you seek new experiences, you're definitely going to learn a thing or two about yourself. Sometimes, it takes a change of environment, or a change of routines, to gain a new perspective on your strengths, weaknesses, emotions, and overall character. Exploring new things is a way of stretching your limits and stepping out of your comfort zone. One of the commonest methods of seeking new experiences is traveling. When you travel, you get to meet people from different cultures, and their way of life might force you to look at yourself in a new light. Traveling also has a calming effect on your mind and can promote clarity of thought.

Meditate

A favorite exercise of yogis, meditation is truly a great practice for increasing your self-awareness. The premise behind meditation is that achieving a calm mental state multiplies your odds of reaching your goals. The classic yoga pose is made by sitting on a firm surface and placing each foot on the opposing thigh. Then you have to perform a breathing exercise that is aimed at eliminating the noise off of your mind. Meditation increases your ability to focus on your internal facets and thus helps you attain a clear understanding of the person that you are.

Reflect on your life

Get in the habit of taking stock of your life. This practice should be done on a daily basis. For instance, you may elect to reflect upon the day's events before you sleep. This will help you identify the areas where you have performed well, underperformed, or outright tanked. It will grant you the insight to sharpen your weak areas and capitalize on your strengths.

Keep a journal

Get in the habit of writing down the various emotional states that you go through during the day, as well as their triggers. This will help you assess your emotional nature, and more importantly, it will put a timeline to your emotional states.

Ask for feedback

As much as you may not want to admit it, sometimes people see things in you that you cannot see yourself. And so, you may want to hear what these people think about you, but take care that you ask people who have your best interests, people who want to see you make progress. When you solicit people's opinions, you make yourself vulnerable because their feedback might hurt you. But you should be open-minded enough to allow criticism, as this is the only way to grow. With the right feedback, you will realize the areas that you have to work on.

Know your emotional triggers

Emotions are merely the brain's way of trying to pass across an important message. There are certain things and events that cause the brain to activate the correlating emotion. It is critical to understand the various causes of your emotions. If you have gone through trauma, obviously you are emotionally scarred. Whenever you come across an event that is even loosely associated with the trauma, the bad emotions come rushing back. For instance, if you were once sexually assaulted on a dark road at night, you might find yourself getting anxious every time you're walking along isolated and lightless paths. Becoming aware that this anxiety is merely a warning that your brain is trying to send might help calm you down.

Set boundaries

You have to learn to set boundaries to develop your self-awareness. Setting boundaries is a way of respecting your time and showing people that you have goals to achieve. It regulates your behavior and guides you in the best manner possible. Setting boundaries and following through with the implementation takes courage and the support of other people. It is one of the critical things in understanding your limits.

Avoid being narrow-minded

A narrow-minded person hardly sees the sense in what other people say, thus closing off any chance to expand their knowledge. However, if you want to increase your self-awareness, you must learn to open up your mind. There are various things you can learn about yourself if only you're open-minded. This is critical especially when it comes to accepting parts of yourself that you consider unbecoming. With an open mind, you also get to change your way of thinking and free yourself from frustrations.

Chapter 7: How to Know if you're Emotionally Intelligent

When you start working on raising your EQ, you will notice that you get stronger in certain aspects of your life. So, how can you tell if this quality is getting stronger in you? Here are some key signs that you are gaining emotional intelligence.

You Follow through on your Word: Emotionally intelligent individuals do not bother claiming things that aren't true. Their word is important to them, and they always follow through on the promises they make to others around them.

Human Behavior Fascinates you: People with a high EQ are intrigued by the behavior of humans. They pay attention to cues such as dialect, body language, and personality idiosyncrasies. Watching people help them discover what it is about others that makes them unique.

You are Okay with your Past: The emotionally intelligent are able to move on from difficulties, facing life in the present moment. If you're too busy for regret and don't waste time ruminating on the past, it's a sign of a high EQ.

You Know your Faults and Strengths: If you have a high EQ, you aren't afraid to admit your shortcomings since you know this is key to improving them. Instead of getting down about their faults, they use them as motivation to get even better and continually improve.

The Future doesn't Scare you: Emotionally intelligent people never bother obsessing about events in the future that haven't occurred yet. They don't need to try to predict the details of every little event, because they enjoy life as it is. Instead of rushing through life to get to the next big thing, they are the active experiencers of their own lives.

When you're Upset, you Know Why: With a high EQ, you don't let doubts and fears come in and take over your mind. You are an active explorer of your own environment and thoughts, finding reasons why your emotions are there and how you can use them.

You are Great at Listening: If you're emotionally intelligent, you know how to listen. You don't just wait for your turn to talk, but actually relate to what the person speaking to you is saying, asking questions to show that you are engaged.

You are Fair at Work and your Personal Life: You have a strong set of morals that you stick to, no matter what. Although values and morals differ from emotionally intelligent person to emotionally intelligent person, they all have high standards of excellence.

You Enjoy Helping Others: If you enjoy helping people without needing a reason, it's a sign of a high EQ. You don't look at a situation where someone needs a hand and automatically wonder what's in it for you but get joy out of being able to help for the sake of helping itself.

You are Good at Reading Emotional Cues: People with a high EQ are able to interpret nonverbal language, gestures, and facial expressions. They know how to look beyond words for the meaning in what someone is saying and how to interpret those signals effectively. This makes them great communicators.

Your Motivation comes from Within you: If you know how to build lasting motivation, you probably have a high EQ. Instead of getting caught up on the end result and losing sight of the process, you know how to enjoy the entire journey, seeing each step as necessary and important. You never want to miss out on chances to learn, because they are happening all the time.

You can say "No": If you have a hard time saying no to people, your emotional intelligence could need some work. It's impossible to please everyone and do everything at once, so setting time aside to prioritize your goals is important.

If you answered yes to any or all of these questions, congratulations! You're doing great at raising your EQ. Remember that you can always improve in this area, and that the journey is never over. If you still have a way to go, refer back to the tips in this book.

Chapter 8: Connection Between Delayed Gratification and Emotional Intelligence

In the 60s, renowned psychologist Walter Mischel did an experiment to observe how four-year-olds controlled their impulses. He put the children in a room and offered each a marshmallow. But there was a hook. He stated that he'd be going out to run an errand and that when he comes back, he will give another marshmallow to the children who don't eat their first marshmallow; however, it was still okay if they choose to not wait for him and eat their first marshmallow anyway.

After he stepped out, most of the kids started feasting on their marshmallow. But a small percentage of the children resisted the urge to eat their marshmallow and chose to wait for Mischel to come back and give them another. In the meantime, these kids performed various activities to avoid temptation, like walking around the room, covering their eyes, putting their heads down, and singing.

Many years later, when the children were in high school, remarkable differences were found between the two groups. The kids who had shown restraint over their impulses seemed more socially confident and well-adjusted compared to their low-willed counterparts. On the side of academics, the kids who held out scored an average of 210 points higher in their SAT.

What can be inferred in this experiment is that there's a huge correlation between delayed gratification and achieving success.

Hard work

In this era of seeking instant thrills, it can be hard to get anyone to invest the time and resources required to achieve a desired outcome. Many people tend to seek the easy way out, and this usually leads to mediocrity. However, a person who can reign in their impulses is much more likely to invest the time and resources to achieve the desired outcome.

Learning to keep from gratifying your every want will instill in you a sense of discipline. For instance, when you challenge yourself into making the best of your income opportunities, you will have an appreciation for your money, and you might be able to see the advantage of saving over mindless spending.

Hard work teaches you how to prioritize and set goals. When you work within that framework, you tend to achieve more and become mindful of your habits. It takes a combination of various productive habits to eventually realize success.

Motivation

In today's society, there's too much noise. Everywhere you turn, someone is trying to get your attention and distract you from what you're doing. Most people find it hard to stay "hungry" for their goals. They get carried away by other thrills. But a person who can manage their urges is in a position to keep fighting for their goals, as they know too well what they stand to gain. Since they have an understanding of this pleasant feeling and the sense of fulfillment that awaits them on the other side, it motivates them to carry on in their pursuit of success.

Healthy lifestyle

If your health is failing, it can be difficult or outright impossible to achieve your goals. While deteriorating health is caused by factors both within and without our control, taking your health in your hands is a major step that asks for commitment on your part. For instance, if you have an alcohol problem, it can be difficult to give it up, and it will thus keep compromising your health. But if you have it in you to delay gratification, you will understand the long-term importance of giving up your alcohol habit. This mentality sets you up for success.

Improved finances

Most people lack financial discipline. That is why they spend their hard-earned money on things that they don't really need and end up burying themselves in debt. Poor financial decisions obviously affect the quality of an individual's life, and there's the possibility of what we call, "Financial ruin." However, a person who's mastered the art of delaying gratification will prioritize their needs. Their money only ever goes into what they really need, and such habits shield them from getting bogged down by debts or straying into financial graves. People who have a hold on their feelings are in a much better position to advance financially.

Gratitude

It can be difficult to show gratitude if you're used to instant thrills and taking the easy way out. Actually, people who like having it easy tend to be entitled. On the other hand, people who can delay their gratification tend to show gratitude to both themselves and other people. This is because they achieve their goals by making plans and putting in the effort. For instance, such people tend to have a great appreciation for their money, and they ensure that they are careful about the things that they buy. They also appreciate people who commit resources to their projects, e.g., employees.

Sense of fulfillment

If you constantly make poor decisions, it doesn't necessarily mean that you're not aware of what you're doing. Most people are. For instance, if you decide against paying your child's school fee so that you can acquire your favorite item, you obviously know that you have done poorly. These bad habits tend to compound, and the resultant guilt can crush your soul. But a person who can control their impulse is careful about the decisions they make, financially or otherwise. In the end, it gives them a sense of fulfillment just knowing they took the best decision that there was.

Good leadership

Success doesn't have to be one-dimensional. For a leader, the real measure of success is not when they reach their goals – it's when their followers reach their goals. As a leader, you have to be able to set good examples. This calls for great self-awareness and consideration on your part. When you set a good example, your followers can adapt to your ways and thus create an enabling environment for accomplishment. It takes a person who can delay gratification to lead by example.

Chapter 9: How emotional intelligence can make you more productive

Emotional intelligence can be quite beneficial in making us more productive, purposeful and provide us with a sense of direction. Being emotionally intelligent opens your mind to the abounding opportunities which you can tap into. Emotional intelligence improves the quality of life you lead and helps you create more productive interpersonal and professional relationships. Here are the benefits of emotional intelligence which you should never miss out on; find out how emotional intelligence can make you more productive.

1. Mastering Emotional responses

Emotional intelligence makes you cognizant of your emotions so that you can control the responses you give to situations that trigger these emotions. When you master your emotions and emotional responses, you become less vulnerable to counterproductive reactions and unstable moods. Letting stress, anxiety, and anger control take hold of you makes it difficult to think rationally and this can affect your productivity both at work and everywhere else. When you are emotionally intelligent, you become aware of possible emotional responses and place them under immediate control.

2. Promoting Self-care and stress/anxiety management

Every day, you are faced with one difficult situation or another which requires you to make some really tough decisions. Sometimes, you have to overwork yourself just to achieve more and be productive. However, this can be quite counterproductive to do. Emotional intelligence trains you to recognize your limits and stay within the boundaries of these limits. Being emotionally intelligent means taking a more proactive approach to situations and also taking proactive breaks when necessary. This prevents you from overstressing yourself or having an emotional breakdown which can quite affect your productivity. Emotional intelligent helps you get more done so as to avoid getting burned out or tapping out. An emotionally intelligent person knows working longer hours won't make them more productive so they take a more proactive approach to achieve productivity.

3. Improving Team Collaborations

Emotional intelligence improves your ability to collaborate with others and work in groups. People who are emotionally intelligent are great at collaborating with others and collaborative efforts are usually more productive. Emotional intelligence makes it easy to read, analyze, and process the emotions, strengths, and weaknesses of others and this can help you devise better ways to achieve productive results. Since empathy is a core skill in emotional intelligence, you also find it easier to put yourself in place of others and determine how they might react to a situation. This makes for great adaptability skills i.e. you find it easy to adapt to any environment you find yourself. It also means you find it easier to make logical and required sacrifices for the group which makes your effort even more productive. Good communication, trust, and value always abound in a group where emotionally intelligent people are.

4. Improving Critique-handling ability

Whether harsh, negative, or positive, emotional intelligence help you handle criticism better. The most emotionally intelligent people usually go out of their way to receive feedback and incorporate it to improve the quality of their work or personal relationships. As an emotionally intelligent person, you never stake criticism personally; instead, you make use of every critique to work harder and make an improvement on yourself. As an emotionally intelligent person, if someone says you are prone to anger, you don't explode in their face thereby proving their point; rather, you accept their submission and then look inward to yourself, see if it's true, and make changes to improve. Emotional intelligence also teaches you to give your own feedback to people i.e. if someone does something to wrong you, you make them know immediately instead of keeping it in.

5. Increasing receptivity to change

No one knows change is necessary and required more than an emotionally intelligent individual. Since emotional intelligence enables self-awareness and promotes self-care, it gives you the required tools to initiate change and also deal with any change you find in your way. There is no point in facing change with a negative mindset and this is exactly what you learn with emotional intelligence. Many people tend to welcome change with nasty attitudes and indifference; this makes it impossible for them to initiate or advocate for change even when it is absolutely necessary. Emotional intelligence gives you a positive outlook that helps you welcome change whether it is desired or not. As someone who is emotionally intelligent, you will even encourage others to embrace positivity and inspire yourself to embrace it too. Change, whether personal or social, becomes much easier when you develop and improve your emotional intelligence skills.

6. Building and Maintaining Valuable Relationships

The relationship you have with others should be one that impacts the quality of life you live positively. There is no point having relationships that add nothing to you and this is something all emotionally intelligent people know. People should be in your life because they add value to you and you reciprocate the gesture. Being emotionally intelligent helps you decipher people fast enough to know if they are the type you want in your life or not. However, it is not enough to simply build quality and valuable relationships; you must also strive to maintain the relationship you have built with others. Emotional intelligence provides you with the cognizance you need to maintain your valuable relationships and do away with the toxic ones.

As a person, it is possible to have low emotional intelligence but with practice and consistency, you can develop your emotional intelligence skills. People with low emotional quotient tend to go through tougher challenges than people with high EQ since they have no idea how to manage their emotions or relationship with others. To live a life of direction, it is highly beneficial to learn and embrace every emotional intelligence skill there is.

Chapter 10: Mindfulness, visualization, guided imagery, and relaxation techniques for instant relief from stress, anxiety, and anger

Mindfulness meditation, visualization, and guided imagery are all relaxation techniques you can use to keep your calm whenever you feel some turmoil within. So, one by one, let's check out how you can practice each of these techniques for relaxation.

Mindfulness

Mindfulness is a quality inherent in all of us but we don't know how to channel it. Thankfully, experts have developed meditation techniques targeted at helping you achieve mindfulness which is the ability to become so in tune with you, your emotions, and your environment.

- Firstly, find a quiet and calm spot in your home or anywhere else you deem quite enough to fully appreciate nature. This place should be tidy, without any form of clutter. Ensure there are lights on whether natural or electronic. You may also sit outside but make sure there is nothing to distract you.

- Next, assume a sitting position in the right posture. It is important to sit in the right posture so as to ensure concentration and minimal distraction. Find a suitable spot to sit, be it a chair, a bench, or a meditation cushion. The sitting spot should be stable, solid, and stationary. Ensure you are aware of your legs and how they are positioned. If you are on a cushion, place your legs comfortably in a crossed position. If you are on a chair, ensure your feet are touching the bare ground. Sit in a straight position without stiffening your body. Let your arms be positioned in a parallel position to your upper body; your hands should be on the top of your legs. Finally, ensure you lower your eyelids so that your gaze falls slightly downwards. Remain in this sitting position for some seconds and relax your body.

- Focus on your breath and the sensations you feel in your body. As you breathe in and breathe out, feel your breath and focus on the sound. Notice everything from the air leaving your body through the nose or mouth to the air entering the body; the rise and fall of your tummy and chest. Make a mental note of every breath you take, in and out. As you do this, take note that your attention will eventually shift from your breath to other things. Have no worry; mindfulness has nothing to do with the elimination of thoughts. Simply return your attention to your breathing each time you notice your thoughts wander.

- In case you need to adjust your posture or physical position, pause your breath before you do this. Whether it is something as simple as moving your hand or scratching your hair, pause. Ensure you do this with intent, leave a space between what you are currently doing and what you need to do.

- Again, your mind will wander over and over to other things; this is normal. However, do not try to engage these thoughts because they will make you lose your concentration totally. Instead, bring your mind back every time it wanders to something else.

- Do this for about 10 minutes and when you are ready, lift your gaze from the ground and open your eyes if they are closed. For a minute, listen to your environment and notice any sound. Listen to your thoughts and emotions. Now, take a decision and determine how you'd like to spend the rest of your day at that moment.

There, you are done. Mindfulness is just as easy as that although you will find it's not as simple in practice. Concentration is key and it is usually so easy to lose your focus.

Visualization

Over the years, visualization has been used to achieve calm, relaxation, and relief from stress, anxiety, and depression. It is a simple case of using images in your head to project yourself to a place you'd like to be; a place of calm till your body itself becomes calm. Some people even consider visualization to be a form of superpower they can use to achieve anything they want. People often regard visualization and guided imagery to be the same but they aren't. Guided imagery is great for stress relief while visualization is more effective for achieving a set goal. You should too! Here is how to practice visualization.

- Find a comfortable and quiet sitting corner without distractions. Take your seat, close your eyes and prepare yourself to imagine what you'd like. It's just like looking at yourself using a different eye. Note that visualization is best practiced when you just wake up or when you are about to retire to bed. This is when you are most relaxed and when your mind is most free.

- Now, visualize an image of yourself sitting in a movie theater with the lights dimmed. The movie starts and there is an image of you being the best version of yourself on the screen. Include as many details as possible; your clothes, emotion, facial expression, physical movements, the environment, and every other important detail. Try to make yourself experience whatever feelings you think you want to experience in this visualized version of yourself. For example, if you are practicing visualization to reduce your anger; project an image of a much calmer version of yourself.

- Next, stand up, take a walk to the screen, open an imagined door, and enter into the movie of yourself. Now you can live and experience everything from inside yourself. This strengthens the effect of the visualization process. Spend as much time as you need to take in all the details; hear the sound and feel the emotions.

- Once you are done, walk out of the screen which still has that image of you, and return to your theater seat. Sit for a while, then grab the screen and crumple in your hands until only a smaller version remains. Take this in your mouth and swallow it. As you swallow, imagine that is the project better, calm, and well-behaved version of yourself being ingested into every cell and vein in your body. Finally, imagine the ingested screen lighting up your body and feel yourself become a pro at controlling your feelings of anger and handling emotions better.

- Finish up and go about your daily business with an improved mindset.

Make visualization practice a part of your everyday routine and watch as life becomes better.

Guided Imagery

This is a highly effective technique for stress and anxiety management which you can practice every day to relieve yourself of stress and other uncomfortable emotions. It has to do with picturing a person, object, event, or memory that makes you feel calm, relaxed, and happy. To do guided imagery, you have to concentrate on all five senses.

- Find a quiet place without noise or distraction. Close your eyes and deeply breathe in and out to relax your mind.

- Once your mind and body are relaxed, visualize yourself in a calm and tranquil environment of your choice. This place may be imagined or real, from a happy memory. It could be your ideal holiday location. The environment should hold strong, emotional meaning to you.

- Ensure you use all five senses in the visualization of this place. If it is by the sea, hear the rush of the waves and feel the sand. Immerse yourself completely into the environment.

- Now, take your time and relax. Spend as much time as

you want in this place, breathing in and out slowly and
deeply.

- Once you are done and ready to leave, project your mind
  back to your current location. You will feel an instant
  calmness, a holdover your emotions, and a refreshing
  energy which makes you feel like you can achieve just
  about anything.

Chapter 11: Guidelines on Managing and Expressing Your Emotions

Emotions are powerful biological forces that we cannot manipulate consciously. Once emotions get involved, things become complicated. Here are some important tips to adhere to to manage and express your emotions appropriately.

Learn to distract yourself

An emotionally intelligent person is aware of his emotional makeup; i.e., how their body responds to various stimuli. At the onset of an unpleasant emotion, rather than entertain it, learn to distract yourself. For instance, if you were working on a serious academic project and a very attractive person of the opposite sex stumbled by, you might get aroused and experience passionate feelings. Well, sexual emotion is not bad in and of itself, but considering that you're doing an important academic project, you might want to banish that sexual emotion.

You can achieve that by distracting yourself – engaging your mind in other activities. You may not have the ability to decide which emotion to experience, but when you pay less attention to a particular emotion, it tends to subside. However, if you lend your attention to a particular emotion, you tend to fuel it and end up increasing its potency.

Never react immediately

Whenever you experience a massive emotional trigger, be careful not to give an immediate response. This will give you time to assess the real situation and come up with the perfect plan. When you give an immediate emotional response, chances are the outcome will be less than desirable. For instance, if the actions or words of a person have triggered your anger, don't erupt in an outburst. This will get your aggressor worried about your next move. Meanwhile, you can be devising your comeback plan, or choose not to do anything at all. When you're consumed by an overpowering urge to give an emotionally-charged response, both your heartbeat and breathing rate will go up. Learning to control your breath can help in regaining your calm.

Have a healthy outlet

In as much as you have to practice restraint where your emotions are concerned, it is also important to have an outlet lest you become an irritable person. When you bottle up emotions inside, you risk having it burst out one day, and woe unto the person on the receiving end. Obviously, this would defeat the purpose of practicing restraint considering that you have overreacted. One of the best outlets for your emotions is engaging in a physically-taxing activity like exercising and training.

Keep the big picture in mind

If you fail to get a handle on your emotions, you run the risk of throwing the baby out with the bathwater. Sometimes, you may get stuck in an unpleasant situation and feel like letting your emotions explode. Try to be wise enough to keep the bigger picture in mind. First ask yourself, what's your agenda? And how are your actions helping that agenda? For instance, say your teenage daughter is driving you up the wall. If you become hostile with her, she may end up cutting off ties with you, thus killing off any chance of you getting to guide her through life.

Communicate well

It doesn't matter what your intentions are, but if you cannot get around to communicating well, you'll have little chance of making progress. For instance, if you are agitated and have to face someone to resolve an issue, your verbal and nonverbal cues will play a critical role in how your message will be taken. Use a pleasant tone and ensure that you engage in active listening. Regardless of how powerful your emotions might be, there are always the right words to capture perfectly what you feel.

Practice honesty

Honesty is indeed the best policy. What's the purpose of expressing yourself in the first place if you're not going to be honest about how you feel? You should at all times ensure that you communicate your emotions in a manner that's as honest as possible, simply because that is the best way for you to get an honest reply. For instance, if someone at work did or said something that left you with a bad taste in your mouth, you might want to walk up to them and express how their actions or words made you feel. How they react is not in your power, but when you take the initiative, you will at least be on the right path to making things right again.

Master the art of timing

When you are pressed emotionally, being considerate is the last thing on your mind. You are simply dying to let the other person know what you're feeling. Emotions have a way of pushing all our wrong buttons, causing us to become impulsive in our decisions, and before we know it, it is over just as quickly as it began. Then we are stuck with the consequences. But, to communicate your emotions meaningfully, you have to ensure that the timing is right.

For instance, if your boss has done something that has triggered you, the last thing you should do is to storm into his office when he's in the middle of a meeting with other high-rank officials. You want to make sure that the environment in which you're communicating your emotions is an enabling one. This increases your odds of achieving the outcome you had planned.

Practice mindfulness
Learn to stay aware of what is going on in your environment. This can only be achieved through mindfulness. When you get in the habit of being interested in other people, you create avenues for channeling positive emotions. We live in a world of pain, and so many people are in need of kindness. It is through mindfulness that we get to show our positive feelings to the world.

Spend time in nature
Our environment has a big effect on our emotional states. If we live or work in chaotic places, our emotions are more or less going to take on that tone. Taking time to be surrounded by nature has a calming effect on your emotions. You could take walks in nature parks, hike, or hunt in the forest. This could help raise your spirits and release all the bad emotions.

Chapter 12: All About NLP

The neuro component focuses on neurology, linguistic refers to language, and programming is about using neural language functions. NLP, in other words, means learning the language of your mind. Isn't that an interesting thing?

Created in the 1970s in California by Richard Bandler and John Grinder, NLP courses are now introduced in seminars and by companies looking to train their managers to enhance their skills in communication and better governance.

What are the benefits of NLP?

Before we move into the techniques and practices of NLP, it is also wise to explore the benefits of NLP in both life, work, and relationships. Here is a breakdown of what you can expect when you go through NLP courses:

In your career:

- By knowing your goals and staying focused on them, you will eventually develop an edge on your competition in business – this can safely and systematically increase your profits.

- If you manage a team, you will learn to effectively manage your internal mindset so that it can positively influence the people you work with, eventually forming a happy and conducive working environment for your entire team to enable them to achieve the team goals.

- NLP also helps you overcome hurdles that may prevent you from taking your career or your business to the next level of greatness.

- You will also learn to motivate yourself as well as the people around you, especially at times of crisis.

- By using a better way to communicate, you will create greater elegance and precision so that you and your team can get what you want to attain your goals.

- You will also learn to think better, be more focused, have better clarity and make constructive decisions.

In your life:

- NLP practice and techniques enable you to connect with yourself and your relationships in a more enriching way.

- You will also be open to more learning possibilities, be more adapted to the changes happening in your life and learn as life moves on.

- Your ability to immediately identify and push through your limitations will also increase. You will also gain a higher momentum of motivation to continue pursuing your business objectives as well as your life mission. Once you break through these limitations, both your life and business will never be the same again as it will change for the better.

- NLP will also train you to master your unconscious mind to learn more quickly than conventional teaching methods allow.

- As you continue practicing NLP, you also learn plenty of things about yourself that you never knew and also discover skills you never thought you had, and increase the creative side of your brain.

- Along the way, you will be more adept at steering your emotions, so they do not get the better of you. You will learn to handle your emotions according to the situation you are in.

- Become a more effective and powerful communicator because you now have a vital edge.

- Your personal relationships will be enhanced as you get better at empathizing and understanding a person's perspective of scenarios.

- You will also work towards increasing your confidence and self-esteem.

Understanding NLP

Just to reinforce the concept of NLP again, let's take a look at another scenario. Imagine trying to communicate with someone who doesn't speak your language and can't understand you no matter how hard you try to explain things – it's like trying to order a dish in a foreign country where you don't speak the language. What we order and what actually comes to our table are two different things.

This is the kind of partnership that most of us have with our unconscious mind. We think something, but what happens, in reality, is a different story altogether. In the practice of NLP, the conscious mind is the goal-setter, whereas the unconscious mind is the goal-getter. The unconscious mind should not be seen as a troublemaker. It is there to get you what you want in life – your goals, tasks, and needs. However, if you do not know how to communicate with what you want in life, then the result is often the opposite of what you desire.

In short, NLP is a personal development tool that is created to help people have better relationships with themselves and the people around them in the pursuit of their goals and happiness – to ultimately lead a more meaningful life.

Practical Exercises to Enhance Your Emotional Intelligence

Speaking of practices and techniques, here are some of the more practical ones that you can try on your own to build EQ using NLP practices:

#1 Dissociation

Dissociation is the technique of identifying an emotion or feeling that makes us feel nervous or fearful and removing it entirely. You may have been in a situation where you suddenly have a bad feeling, but this isn't about instinct or gut feeling. Rather, the experience just mentally breaks you down, such as giving a speech in front of people or even taking the elevator alone (some people feel uncomfortable being in a small space). Maybe you suddenly retract from conversations when you feel surrounded by people? These feelings may seem like a normal reaction, but while it is okay to feel this way sometimes, it can be chronic if it starts interfering in life and work. The dissociation technique helps to overcome this feeling and involves:

- Identifying the emotions that you want to overcome.

- Imagine yourself floating out of your body to look at yourself and look at the entire scenario from an observer's point of view.

- Notice how you feel.

- Imagine flowing out of your body again, so you are looking at yourself, looking at yourself. This double take on dissociation usually gets rid of any negative emotion from a minor situation.

#2 Content Reframing

This technique is extremely useful whenever we feel helpless or when negative thoughts and emotions come weighing down at us. Reframing basically involves taking a negative situation and empowering yourself by changing the meaning that you associate the experience with, subsequently turning it into a positive experience.

It starts with:

- Identifying the negative scenario such as a divorce. Divorces are never easy but let's reframe it.

- What are the positive outcomes of being divorced? You can now look at other relationships. You can also look forward to forming a better relationship with the next person since you have learned valuable lessons. You have the freedom to do the things you couldn't do while being in the previous relationship.

- You have taken a negative scenario and reframed it to give yourself an entirely different experience.

- Shifting your focus to more positive aspects just helps you have better clarity; thus, enabling you to make better decisions.

#3 Anchoring

As described earlier, anchoring is a very significant and commonly used NLP technique. Anchoring is best described as a neurological association between a sound, scenario or situation and the behavior we have when we come face-to-face with that situation. It is also known as a conditioned response. In NLP, it is simply described as anchoring yourself to these situations.

Anchoring helps us have a desired positive emotional response when we face a certain sensation. When we choose a positive emotion or thought, and connect it deliberately to a simple gesture, we also trigger the anchor whenever we feel negative emotions. This technique is meant to change our emotions immediately. It involves:

- Starting with identifying how we want to feel whether it is calmness or happiness or even confidence.

- Deciding where this feeling should be placed to anchor our body. It can be a small place like our earlobe or even clasping our fingers, rubbing our palms or simply touching our knuckles. The physical action allows us to trigger our positive sensations at will. It doesn't matter where this physical action is as long as when you do it, it is unique to you and you know what it means.

- Go back into your past at a time when you felt that state of feeling and mentally float your body to the time you felt most confident or happy or calm. Look at this scenario through your own eyes and relive that memory. Slowly adjust your body language so that it matches that memory. Experience what you see and hear what you heard back in this memory as well as the feeling that came into you.

- This experience is the same as recollecting a funny joke or story from the past and the feelings you felt and the memories you experienced. Anchoring is getting into this experience and feeling the happiness you felt.

- Cling as much as you can onto this memory through touching, pulling and squeezing the part of your body of your choosing. Release from the touch when the emotional state peaks and starts wearing off.

- What you are doing is creating a neurological stimulus-response which will trigger the state of emotions whenever you touch yourself at the spot again. Whether it is confidence or happiness or calmness, touching this spot again will trigger your positive responses.

- To enhance the memory or response trigger, think of another memory that you felt and relive it again by going through this anchoring practice again. Each time you add your anchor of positive feelings, the trigger will be stronger.

#4 Creating Better Rapport

This NLP technique is easy but extremely powerful to help get along with just about anyone. While there are plenty of ways to build rapport, this NLP technique is the most effective, not to mention the quickest. It involves mirroring, very subtly, the other person's body language and tone of voice. Easy but needs to be done with extreme subtlety – that you can almost consider it art. People generally like other people who are like themselves – birds of a feather flock together anyway. By mirroring the other person's actions, the brain gives off mirror neurons, which are pleasure sensors that give people the sense of liking someone that is mirroring them.

Here's what you need to do:

- Stand or sit the way the other person is standing or sitting. Tilt your head the same way.

- Smile when they smile. Mirror their facial expressions and their body language.

- The idea here is to do it as unconsciously and subtly as

possible.

Do not be too overt as then it may seem like you are merely copying them and this will break rapport. Mirror people in a calm and natural way.

#5 Influence and Persuasion

NLP practices are especially dedicated to helping people to manage conflict, eliminate negative emotions, as well as do away with limiting beliefs. A small portion of NLP, though, is dedicated to influencing and persuading other people.

Milton H. Erickson, a mentor in the NLP field who is also a psychiatrist, studied the subconscious mind using hypnotherapy – the scientific line not the entertainment kind. Erickson was adept at hypnosis, and he also created a way to speak to the subconscious minds of people without even needing hypnotism. He could also hypnotize people at any given time. This method that Erickson used became known as Conversational Hypnosis.

Conversational hypnosis is a powerful tool that can be used to not only persuade and influence people but also to help people overcome fears, manage conflicts, stop limiting beliefs and raise conscious awareness.

www.ingramcontent.com/pod-product-compliance
Lightning Source LLC
Chambersburg PA
CBHW020935160726
47993CB00007B/2795